VEGETARIAN
Pasta
RECIPES

A QUANTUM BOOK

Published by
Chartwell Books
A Division of Book Sales, Inc.
114 Northfield Avenue
Edison, New Jersey, 08837
USA

ISBN 0-7858-0674-1

This book was produced by
Quantum Books Ltd
6 Blundell Street
London N7 9BH

Produced in Australia by Griffin Colour

VEGETARIAN
Pasta
RECIPES

CHARTWELL
BOOKS, INC.

Pasta Dough

This is the basic recipe referred to throughout the book. The dough can be made up to 2 days in advance, if kept airtight in the fridge. Bring the dough to room temperature before rolling out.

Freezing pasta is best done after it has been rolled out and cut into the required shape. Cook from frozen, allowing a little extra cooking time for stuffed pasta shapes.

MAKES ABOUT 1¼ LB

3 cups all-purpose flour
1 tbsp salt
4 tbsp sunflower oil
1 tbsp water
3 eggs

1

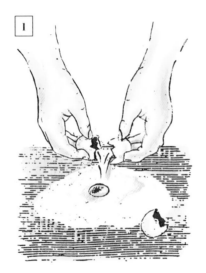

In a large mixing bowl, combine the flour and salt. Make a well in the center. In a small bowl, combine the sunflower oil and water and beat well. Break the eggs into the well, and add the oil and water mixture gradually. Mix until the dough forms clumps.

2

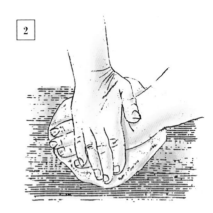

Turn out onto a lightly floured surface and knead the dough for about 5 minutes, adding the minimum amount of extra flour to stop the dough sticking, if necessary.

Place the dough in a plastic bag or seal in plastic wrap and leave to rest, at room temperature, for at least 30 minutes.

3

Roll out the dough, and cut to any shape you require.

TIPS FOR COOKING PERFECT PASTA:

- Use good-quality pasta.

- Use a saucepan that is large enough to hold the pasta with the water and still have at least one third of the saucepan free.

- Bring the water to the boil before adding the pasta, then simmer for the duration of the cooking time.

- Add a dash of oil to the cooking water to help prevent the pasta sticking together.

- Cook the pasta until *al dente,* or until just tender.

- To halt the cooking process, drain the pasta through a sieve and rinse under cold running water.

These basic sauces are used in recipes throughout the book. However, they can also be used as recipes in their own right, poured over or mixed into your favorite pasta shapes. Made up to two days in advance and kept, covered in the refrigerator, the sauces can be reheated for use in the recipes.

Cheese Sauce

This sauce will keep in the fridge for up to a week. Use for lasagnes, bakes, toppings, and fillings.

MAKES ABOUT 2½ CUPS

2 tbsp butter or margarine

¼ cup all-purpose flour

2½ cups warm milk

1 tsp Dijon mustard

1½ cups grated mature Cheddar cheese

salt and freshly ground black pepper

Melt the butter or margarine in a medium-sized saucepan, and stir in the flour. Cook for 30 seconds, then remove from the heat.

Stir in the milk, a little at a time, blending well after each addition to prevent any lumps. Return the sauce to a medium heat, and stir constantly until the sauce thickens and boils.

Add the mustard and cheese, and season to taste with salt and freshly ground black pepper. Continue to cook, stirring constantly, until the cheese has melted.

VARIATIONS:

MUSHROOM SAUCE Omit the mustard and cheese, and stir in 6oz/ 1½ cups chopped button mushrooms that have been sautéed in a little olive oil with a clove of crushed garlic and a pinch of dried thyme.

TOMATO SAUCE Omit the mustard and cheese, and stir in 3 tbsp tomato paste.

RAVIOLI

Pesto Sauce

This traditional Italian sauce should be used in moderation as it has a very strong flavor. Delicious stirred into fresh pasta, Pesto Sauce can also be used as an ingredient, added to other sauces and dishes. The texture of the finished pesto can be left relatively coarse or puréed until smooth.

SERVES 4–6

2 cloves of garlic, crushed

8 tbsp chopped, fresh basil

2 tbsp chopped, fresh parsley

scant ½ cup pine nuts

1 cup fresh, grated Parmesan cheese

⅔ cup extra virgin olive oil

salt and freshly ground black pepper

Place all the ingredients in a food processor or blender, and blend until the pesto reaches the desired texture.

Stir Pesto Sauce into freshly cooked pasta tossed in butter and freshly ground black pepper. Serve immediately with extra freshly grated Parmesan cheese.

> **TIP:**
> For a more traditional method of preparation, place all the ingredients in a mortar and use the pestle to grind and pound until the pesto reaches the desired texture.

BASIL

Cream Sauce

An excellent standby sauce for any occasion. It is delicious served with spaghetti, or used as a foundation for other ingredients to make a more elaborate dish.

SERVES 4

2 cloves of garlic, crushed

3 tbsp chopped, fresh parsley

1¼ cups light cream

salt and freshly ground black pepper

Place all the ingredients in a medium-sized frying pan and cook over low heat for 5–8 minutes, stirring occasionally.

> **SERVING SUGGESTION:**
> Stir Cream Sauce into freshly cooked tagliatelle verde, and serve immediately with plenty of freshly grated Parmesan cheese.

PARSLEY

Herby Mushroom Pasta Salad

Any small pasta shapes would be suitable for this dish. It can be served as a filling main course at lunchtime, or as an accompaniment.

SERVES 4–8

1lb dried pasta shapes

dash of olive oil

½lb cup mushrooms, quartered

1 red pepper, deseeded and cut into ½-inch squares

1 yellow pepper, deseeded and cut into ½-inch squares

1 cup pitted black olives

4 tbsp chopped, fresh basil

2 tbsp chopped, fresh parsley

FOR THE DRESSING:

2 tsp red wine vinegar

1 tsp salt

freshly ground black pepper

4 tbsp extra virgin olive oil

1 clove of garlic, crushed

1–2 tsp Dijon mustard

Bring a large saucepan of water to the boil, and add the pasta shapes with a dash of olive oil. Cook for about 10 minutes, stirring occasionally, until tender. Drain, and rinse under cold running water. Drain well again.

Place the cooked pasta shapes in a large salad bowl, and add the remaining salad ingredients. Mix well to combine.

To make the dressing, place all the ingredients in a screw-top jar and shake well. Pour the dressing over the salad and toss together.

Cover and refrigerate for at least 30 minutes, then toss again before serving.

Pasta-topped Mushrooms

This dish is delicious served cold with a crisp, leafy salad, or warm as an appetizer or an accompaniment. The topping can be made in advance and arranged on the mushrooms at the last minute.

SERVES 2–4

¼ cup dried small stellette (stars)

dash of olive oil

4 large flat mushrooms

¼ cup butter

1 clove of garlic, crushed

½ yellow pepper, deseeded and finely diced

½ orange pepper, deseeded and finely diced

generous ¼lb blue cheese, such as Stilton or Danish blue, crumbled

salt and freshly ground black pepper

2 tbsp chopped, fresh parsley

Bring a large saucepan of water to the boil, and add the stellette with a dash of olive oil. Cook for about 7 minutes, stirring occasionally, until tender. Drain and set aside.

Cut the stalks out of the mushrooms and discard. Arrange the mushrooms, stalk side up, on a baking sheet and set aside.

To make the topping, melt the butter in a frying pan, and sauté the garlic for about 2 minutes. Add the diced peppers, and cook for a further 5–7 minutes. Stir in the crumbled blue cheese, and season to taste with salt and freshly ground black pepper. Add the parsley and stellette. Stir well.

Top each mushroom with the pasta mixture, then place the baking sheet in the broiler for 2–5 minutes, or until the topping is lightly golden and the mushrooms are warmed through.

Tagliatelle with Mushrooms

A quick supper for any occasion. Try using spaghetti or linguini for a change.

SERVES 4

1lb dried tagliatelle

dash of olive oil

2 tbsp butter

1 clove of garlic, crushed

2 tbsp chopped, fresh parsley

½lb button or cup mushrooms, sliced

salt and freshly ground black pepper

1¼ cups light cream

freshly grated Parmesan cheese, to serve

Bring a large saucepan of water to the boil, and add the tagliatelle with a dash of olive oil. Cook for about 10 minutes, stirring occasionally, until tender. Drain and set aside.

Meanwhile, melt the butter in a large frying pan, and sauté the garlic and chopped parsley for 2–3 minutes. Add the sliced mushrooms and cook for 5–8 minutes, or until softened and slightly browned.

Season the mushroom mixture with salt and freshly ground black pepper, then stir in the cream. Cook the sauce for 1–2 minutes, then stir in the tagliatelle. Continue to cook while stirring to coat the tagliatelle in the sauce. Serve with plenty of freshly grated Parmesan cheese.

OPPOSITE Pasta-topped Mushrooms

CEP

Fusilli with Wild Mushrooms

Wild mushrooms, or ceps, are increasingly available and are the special ingredient in this dish. Dried ceps can be found in Italian delicatessens; they need to be soaked in water for 30 minutes before using in the recipe.

SERVES 4

¾lb/3½ cups dried long fusilli (twists)

dash of olive oil plus ¼ cup

1 clove of garlic, crushed

2 tbsp chopped, fresh thyme

generous ¼lb shiitake mushrooms, sliced

generous ¼lb oyster mushrooms

½oz dried ceps, soaked, drained, and sliced

salt and freshly ground black pepper

freshly grated Parmesan cheese, to serve

Bring a large saucepan of water to the boil, and add the fusilli with a dash of olive oil. Cook for about 10 minutes, stirring occasionally, until tender. Drain and set aside, covered.

Heat the olive oil in a large frying pan, and add the garlic and fresh thyme. Cook for 1–2 minutes, then stir in all the mushrooms and season to taste with salt and freshly ground black pepper.

Fry the mushroom mixture over high heat for 3–4 minutes to brown slightly, then turn the mixture into the saucepan containing the fusilli. Toss together briefly, then serve with a little freshly grated Parmesan cheese.

FIELD

Cheesy Mushroom Canapés

These tasty morsels are ideal for entertaining. They can be made in advance, and are delicious served with drinks.

CONCHIGLIE

SERVES 8–10

20 dried large lumache rigate or large shells

dash of olive oil

3 tbsp freshly grated Parmesan cheese

FOR THE FILLING:

2 tbsp olive oil

1 clove of garlic, chopped

1 small onion, finely chopped

3 tbsp chopped, fresh parsley

6oz/1½ cups button mushrooms, very finely chopped

⅓ cup pitted olives, very finely chopped

½lb cream cheese

salt and freshly ground black pepper

Bring a large saucepan of water to the boil, and add the pasta with a dash of olive oil. Cook for about 10 minutes, stirring occasionally, until tender. Drain, and rinse under cold running water. Pat dry with paper towels, and set aside.

To make the filling, heat the oil in a large frying pan, and sauté the garlic and onion for about 3 minutes, until softened. Remove from the heat, and stir in the remaining filling ingredients.

Use a teaspoon to stuff each pasta shape with the filling, then arrange them on a baking sheet. Sprinkle with grated Parmesan cheese, and place in the broiler for about 5 minutes until golden. Arrange on a serving platter.

Pinwheel Pasta Bake.

Pinwheel Pasta Bake

This simple, unpretentious dish is perfect for a family supper, and makes a good recipe for the freezer. When thawed, reheat, covered, in a medium-hot oven.

SERVES 4–6

1½lb dried rotelle (pinwheels)

dash of olive oil

2 tbsp sunflower oil

1 clove of garlic, crushed

½lb mushrooms, quartered

¼lb zucchini, chopped

3 tbsp chopped, fresh parsley

⅔ cup vegetable broth

2¼ cups grated mature Cheddar cheese

Bring a large saucepan of water to the boil, and add the rotelle with a dash of olive oil. Cook for about 10 minutes, sitrring occasionally, until tender. Drain, and set aside.

Heat the sunflower oil in a large frying pan, and sauté the garlic for 2 minutes. Add the mushrooms and zucchini, and cook, covered, for 5 minutes, or until softened.

Stir the chopped parsley and vegetable broth into the mushroom mixture, and continue to cook, covered, for a further 10 minutes. Add the rotelle, and stir in the grated cheese.

Preheat the oven to 400°F. Transfer the pasta mixture to a deep casserole dish, and bake for about 20 minutes. Serve with warm, crusty bread.

ROTELLE

Hearty Cream of Mushroom Soup

Perfect for a cold winter's night or even a filling lunchtime dish. Serve with warm, crusty garlic bread for a more substantial meal.

SERVES 4

2 tbsp butter

1 onion, finely chopped

¾lb cup mushrooms, finely chopped

1 tbsp all-purpose flour

2½ cups vegetable broth

1¼ cups milk

salt and freshly ground black pepper

½ cup cooked tiny pasta shapes

pinch of freshly grated nutmeg

Melt the butter in a large saucepan, and sauté the onion for about 3 minutes until softened. Add the chopped mushrooms, cover, and cook for a further 5 minutes.

Stir in the flour, then gradually add the broth and milk, stirring well after each addition. Cover, and cook for 15–20 minutes, stirring occasionally. Season with salt and freshly ground black pepper. Stir in the pasta shapes and grated nutmeg. Cook for a final 2–3 minutes, then serve.

Bucatini with Tomatoes

This is a vegetarian version of a simple yet classic Italian dish. Use Parmesan cheese if Pecorino is not available.

YELLOW CHERRY

SERVES 4

¾lb dried bucatini (long tubes)

dash of olive oil

2 cloves of garlic, crushed

1 onion, finely chopped

1lb carton sieved tomatoes

4 tbsp chopped, fresh basil

salt and freshly ground black pepper

butter, for greasing

⅔ cup freshly grated Pecorino or Parmesan cheese

Bring a large saucepan of water to the boil, and add the bucatini with a dash of olive oil. Cook for about 10 minutes, stirring occasionally, until tender. Drain and set aside.

Preheat the oven to 400°F. Place the garlic, onion, sieved tomatoes, basil, and salt and freshly ground black pepper in a large frying pan, and heat until simmering. Cook for about 5 minutes, then remove from the heat.

Arrange the bucatini in a shallow, buttered, ovenproof dish. Curl it around to fit the dish, adding one or two tubes at a time, until the dish is tightly packed with the pasta.

Spoon the tomato mixture over the top, prodding the pasta to ensure the sauce sinks down to the bottom of the dish. Sprinkle with the grated cheese, and bake for 25–30 minutes, until bubbling, crisp, and golden. Cut in wedges, like a cake, to serve.

Tagliatelle Neapolitan

Yellow tomatoes make this dish look particularly attractive, though red ones taste just as good. If you can't find fresh tagliatelle, use the dried egg version.

1lb fresh, multicolored tagliatelle

dash of olive oil, plus 2 tbsp

2 cloves of garlic, crushed

1 onion, chopped

3 tbsp chopped, fresh basil or oregano

1lb yellow and red tomatoes, skinned, deseeded, and chopped

8oz carton sieved tomatoes

salt and freshly ground black pepper

fresh basil, to garnish

freshly grated Parmesan cheese, to serve

Bring a large saucepan of water to the boil, and add the tagliatelle with a dash of olive oil. Cook for about 5 minutes, stirring occasionally, until tender. Drain and set aside, covered.

Heat the remaining oil in a large frying pan, and sauté the garlic, onion, and basil or oregano for about 3 minutes, or until the onion has softened.

Add the chopped tomato flesh and sieved tomatoes, and season with salt and freshly ground black pepper. Stir and cook for about 10 minutes, until thickened and bubbling. Serve with the tagliatelle. Garnish with fresh basil and sprinkle with freshly grated Parmesan cheese.

Fusilli with Sun-dried Tomatoes

A dish that is delicious served warm as a main course or cold as a summer salad. Tomato pesto is widely available.

SERVES 2–4

1lb dried fusilli (twists)

dash of olive oil, plus extra for drizzling

2 tbsp tomato pesto

6oz jar sun-dried tomatoes, drained and chopped

4 plum tomatoes, sliced into wedges

4 tbsp chopped, fresh basil

salt and freshly ground black pepper

Bring a large saucepan of water to the boil, and add the fusilli with a dash of olive oil. Cook for about 10 minutes, stirring occasionally, until tender. Drain and return to the saucepan.

Stir in the remaining ingredients, drizzle with olive oil and serve warm immediately, or cool and refrigerate to serve chilled, if preferred.

OPPOSITE *Fusilli with Sun-dried Tomatoes.*

Spicy Stuffed Tomatoes

Beefsteak tomatoes are perfect for stuffing. Serve as a vegetable accompaniment or as an appetizer. To make the tomatoes stand up in the dish, slice a thin shaving off the bottom of each one.

SERVES 4

½ cup dried pastina (any tiny shapes)

dash of olive oil

4 large beefsteak tomatoes

butter, for greasing

FOR THE FILLING:

2 medium potatoes, cut into ¼-inch cubes

4 tbsp olive oil

2 cloves of garlic, crushed

1 onion, finely chopped

2 tsp mild curry powder

pinch of ground cumin

1 tbsp tomato paste

4 tbsp chopped, fresh coriander

salt and freshly ground black pepper

Bring a saucepan of water to the boil, and add the pastina with a dash of olive oil. Cook for about 8 minutes, stirring occasionally, until tender. Drain and set aside.

Slice the tops off the tomatoes and reserve for the lids. Using a teaspoon, scrape out the flesh of each tomato and reserve. Arrange the hollowed tomatoes in a buttered, oven-proof dish and set aside.

To make the filling, cook the potatoes in boiling water for about 10 minutes, until tender. Drain and set aside. Heat the olive oil in a large frying pan, and sauté the garlic and onion for about 3 minutes, until softened.

Add the curry powder, cumin, and tomato paste. Cook for 2 minutes, then gently stir in the pastina and cooked potato. Add the chopped coriander, and season with salt and freshly ground black pepper. Cook for a further 2–3 minutes, stirring occasionally, then remove from the heat.

Preheat the oven to 400°F. Stuff the tomatoes with the filling, placing any extra in the bottom of the dish. Place the tomato lids on top and bake for about 20 minutes, or until heated through.

BEEFSTEAK

Italian Spaghettini

Italian Spaghettini

Pine nuts give this dish its special taste and texture. Serve it straight from the pan.

PLUM

SERVES 4

1lb dried multicolored spaghettini

dash of olive oil

¼ cup butter

1 clove of garlic, crushed

1 small onion, very finely chopped

⅔ cup pine nuts

8oz carton sieved tomatoes

salt and freshly ground black pepper

4 tbsp chopped, fresh basil

2 tbsp chopped, fresh parsley

Bring a large saucepan of water to the boil, and add the dried spaghettini with a dash of olive oil. Cook for about 10 minutes, stirring occasionally, until tender. Drain, and set aside.

Melt the butter in a large frying pan and sauté the garlic and onion for about 3 minutes, or until the onion has softened. Add the pine nuts and stir-fry until evenly golden.

Add the sieved tomatoes, herbs, and salt and freshly ground black pepper, and cook for about 5 minutes, stirring occasionally.

Add the spaghettini, and stir well to coat in the tomato sauce. Cook for a further 5 minutes, then serve immediately.

Fettuccine with Tomatoes and Mozzarella

This delicious summertime salad can be made well in advance and left to marinate for up to 3 hours.

SERVES 4

¾lb dried egg fettuccine

dash of olive oil

1lb (about 2 medium) beefsteak tomatoes, skinned, deseeded, and sliced

5 tbsp extra virgin olive oil

2 cloves of garlic, crushed

6 tbsp chopped, fresh basil

2 tbsp chopped, fresh oregano

¾lb mozzarella cheese, cut into ½-inch cubes

⅔ cup freshly grated Pecorino or Parmesan cheese

salt and freshly ground black pepper

Bring a large saucepan of water to the boil, and add the fettuccine with a dash of olive oil. Cook for about 10 minutes, stirring occasionally, until tender. Drain and rinse under cold running water. Drain again, and set aside.

In a large bowl, combine the sliced tomato flesh with the remaining ingredients and toss together lightly. Add the cooked fettuccine, and mix lightly to coat in the oil. Serve this salad at room temperature with warm garlic bread.

Tomato Mozzarella Kebabs

These are excellent for a vegetarian barbecue. Serve the kebabs with plenty of hot, crusty garlic bread and salad.

SERVES 4

1¼ cups dried rotelle (pinwheels)

dash of olive oil, plus 4 tbsp

2 cloves of garlic, crushed

salt and freshly ground black pepper

8–12 cherry tomatoes

½lb mozzarella cheese, cut into 1-inch cubes

YELLOW CHERRY

Bring a large saucepan of water to the boil, and add the rotelle with a dash of olive oil. Cook for about 10 minutes, stirring occasionally, until tender. Drain and rinse under cold running water. Drain again and set aside.

In a small bowl, combine the olive oil, garlic, and salt and freshly ground black pepper. Set aside.

To make the kebabs, place one rotelle, a tomato, then a cube of mozzarella cheese onto kebab skewers until all the ingredients have been used. Arrange the skewers on a baking sheet and brush liberally with the garlic olive oil mixture, turning the kebabs to coat evenly.

Place the kebabs in a preheated broiler for 5–7 minutes, turning the skewers halfway through cooking, until browned. Serve immediately.

> **TIP:**
> If using wooden skewers, soak them in water for at least one hour before threading on the kebab ingredients. This will help prevent them from burning during grilling.

Spaghettini with Tomato Ragout

This version of ragout is a brilliant standby sauce to use when hunger won't wait for time.

SERVES 4

1lb dried spaghettini

dash of olive oil

freshly grated Parmesan cheese, to serve

FOR THE RAGOUT:

2 tbsp butter

1 clove of garlic, crushed

1 large onion, finely chopped

14oz can chopped tomatoes

⅔ cup dry red wine

4 tbsp chopped, fresh basil

salt and freshly ground black pepper

Bring a large saucepan of water to the boil, and add the spaghettini with a dash of olive oil. Cook for about 10 minutes, stirring occasionally, until tender. Drain and set aside, covered, to keep warm.

To make the ragout, melt the butter in a large frying pan and sauté the garlic and onion for about 3 minutes, until softened. Add the remaining ragout ingredients, stir, and simmer for 15 minutes, until slightly thickened. Serve with the spaghettini, sprinkled with freshly grated Parmesan cheese.

OPPOSITE *Tomato Mozzarella Kebabs.*

Stuffed Peppers

A refreshing alternative to rice, pasta makes a perfect filling for peppers. Tiny pasta shapes also work well in this dish. Serve with a crisp green salad.

SERVES 4

½lb gnocchetti sardi (small dumpling shapes)

dash of olive oil

4 peppers, for stuffing

flat leaf parsley sprigs, to garnish

FOR THE FILLING:

¼ cup butter

6 scallions, finely chopped

2 cloves of garlic, crushed

1 pepper, deseeded and finely diced

salt and freshly ground black pepper

⅔ cup freshly grated Parmesan cheese

Bring a large saucepan of water to the boil, and add the gnocchetti sardi with a dash of olive oil. Cook for about 10 minutes, stirring occasionally, until tender. Drain and set aside.

Preheat the oven to 400°F. Lay each pepper on its side and slice off the top, reserving it to make the lid. Scoop out and discard the seeds and pith. Arrange the hollowed-out peppers in a shallow, ovenproof dish, and set aside.

To make the filling, melt the butter in a large frying pan and sauté the scallions and garlic for about 2 minutes, then add the diced pepper. Season with salt and freshly ground black pepper and cook for about 5 minutes, stirring occasionally.

Add the gnocchetti and the Parmesan cheese to the filling mixture, and cook for about 2 minutes to heat through. Using a dessertspoon, stuff each pepper with the pasta filling, scattering any extra around the edges.

Place the pepper lids in the dish and bake for about 30 minutes, until the peppers have softened. Just before serving, place in the broiler for 2–3 minutes to char the pepper skins, if desired. Serve garnished with parsley sprigs.

RED

Pepper and Pasta Ratatouille.

Pepper and Pasta Ratatouille

Served with a hot, buttered baked potato, this simple dish is perfectly delicious.

CONCHIGLIE

SERVES 4–6

1lb dried wholewheat gnocchi piccoli (small shells)

dash of olive oil, plus 3 tbsp

2 cloves of garlic, crushed

1 onion, chopped

2 green peppers, deseeded and cut into chunks

14oz can chopped tomatoes

2 heaped tbsp tomato paste

⅔ cup dry red wine

2 tbsp fresh oregano

salt and freshly ground black pepper

fresh oregano sprigs, to garnish

Bring a large saucepan of water to the boil, and add the gnocchi piccoli with a dash of olive oil. Cook for about 10 minutes, stirring occasionally, until tender. Drain and set aside.

Heat the remaining olive oil in a large saucepan and sauté the garlic and onion for about 3 minutes, until softened. Stir in the pepper chunks. Cover and cook for about 5 minutes, or until the pepper has softened slightly.

Stir in the remaining ingredients, except the oregano sprigs, into the pepper mixture and bring to simmering point. Reduce the heat, cover, and cook for about 10 minutes, then stir in the gnocchi piccoli. Cook for a further 5 minutes, stirring occasionally. Serve garnished with fresh oregano sprigs.

Pasta with Pepper Sauce and Olives

This low-fat Pepper Sauce helps to keep the calories in this dish down. As long as the pasta used is dairy-free, this dish is also suitable for vegans.

SERVES 4

4½ cups dried rigatoni (short tubes)

dash of olive oil

⅓ cup pitted black olives, roughly chopped

grated Cheddar cheese, to serve

FOR THE PEPPER SAUCE:

2 red peppers, skinned, deseeded, and roughly chopped

4 cloves of garlic, peeled

1¼ cups vegetable broth

salt and freshly ground black pepper

Bring a large saucepan of water to the boil, and add the rigatoni with a dash of olive oil. Cook for about 10 minutes, stirring occasionally, until tender. Drain and return to the saucepan. Set aside.

To make the sauce, place the chopped pepper, garlic and vegetable broth in a food processor or blender, and season with salt and freshly ground black pepper. Purée until smooth.

Stir the Pepper Sauce into the rigatoni with the chopped olives. Serve with grated Cheddar cheese.

Tortellini, Peppers, and Pine Nut Salad

Red peppers can be used instead of chili peppers, if you prefer. For best results, allow the salad to chill for at least an hour before serving.

SERVES 4–6

scant ¾lb fresh tortellini

dash of olive oil

1 onion, very finely sliced

1 green pepper, deseeded and very finely diced

⅔ cup toasted pine nuts

1 red chili pepper, deseeded and sliced (optional)

4-inch piece of cucumber, very thinly sliced

1 orange, peeled and very thinly sliced

FOR THE DRESSING:

4 tbsp olive oil

2 tbsp sweet soya sauce

2 tbsp vinegar

salt and freshly ground black pepper

Bring a large saucepan of water to the boil, and add the tortellini with a dash of olive oil. Cook for about 4 minutes, stirring occasionally, until tender. Drain and rinse under cold running water. Drain again and set aside.

Place the tortellini in a large mixing bowl and add the remaining salad ingredients. Toss together lightly.

To make the salad dressing, place the ingredients in a screw-top jar and shake well to combine. Pour the dressing over the salad, toss, and serve.

CHILLIES

Rigatoni with Peppers and Garlic

The raw garlic added at the end of the recipe gives this dish the true taste of the Mediterranean.

YELLOW

SERVES 4

¾lb dried rigatoni (large tubes)

dash of olive oil, plus 4 tbsp

1 large onion, chopped

4 cloves of garlic, finely chopped

2 large red peppers, deseeded and roughly chopped

2 large yellow peppers, deseeded and roughly chopped

2 tsp chopped, fresh thyme

salt and freshly ground black pepper

Bring a large saucepan of water to the boil, and add the rigatoni with a dash of olive oil. Cook for about 10 minutes, stirring occasionally, until tender. Drain and set aside.

Heat the remaining oil in a large frying pan. Add the onion, 2 cloves of garlic, peppers, and thyme. Cook over a medium heat for 10–15 minutes, stirring occasionally, until the vegetables are tender and beginning to brown.

Add the pasta shapes to the pepper mixture. Stir in the remaining garlic and seasoning. Serve immediately.

Tortellini, Peppers, and Pine Nut Salad.

Pimento Pasta

A quick store-cupboard
recipe for a last-minute
supper surprise.

S E R V E S 4

¾lb dried spaghettini

dash of olive oil, plus 2 tbsp

2 cloves of garlic, crushed

14oz can red pimento, thinly sliced

salt and freshly ground black pepper

freshly grated Parmesan cheese, to serve
(optional)

Bring a large saucepan of water to the boil, and add the spaghettini with a dash of olive oil. Cook for about 10 minutes, stirring occasionally, until tender. Drain and return to the saucepan. Set aside, covered, to keep warm.

Heat the remaining olive oil in a frying pan, and add the garlic and sliced pimento. Stir-fry for 3–5 minutes, then tip into the warm spaghettini. Stir to combine. Serve with a little freshly grated Parmesan cheese, if desired.

Pasta with Green Peppers and Pesto

If linguini is unavailable, spaghettini or tagliatelle will work just as well in this dish.

TARRAGON

SERVES 4

1lb fresh linguini (thin, flat strips)

dash of olive oil, plus 2 tbsp

2 cloves of garlic, crushed

½ quantity Pesto Sauce (page 10)

¼ cup vegetable broth

1 green pepper, deseeded and very thinly sliced

fresh herbs, to garnish

Bring a large saucepan of water to the boil, and add the linguini with a dash of olive oil. Cook for about 4 minutes, stirring occasionally, until tender. Drain and return to the saucepan. Stir in a dash more olive oil and set aside, covered, to keep warm.

Heat the remaining olive oil in a large frying pan and sauté the garlic for 1–2 minutes, then stir in the Pesto Sauce. Add the vegetable broth, stir, and cook for 1 minute, then add the pepper slices. Cook for a further 7–10 minutes, stirring occasionally, until the pepper has softened. Stir the pepper mixture into the linguini and serve, garnished with fresh herbs.

Fusilli with Roasted Peppers.

Fusilli with Roasted Peppers

To prevent the pasta from sticking together, wash off the starchy cooking liquid by rinsing the pasta under boiling water from the kettle. Continue as directed in the recipe.

SERVES 4–6

1lb dried long fusilli

dash of olive oil

2 yellow peppers, deseeded and cut into chunks

3 cloves of garlic, crushed

¼ cup olive oil

1½ cups grated Cheddar cheese

⅔ cup freshly grated Parmesan cheese

chopped, fresh parsley, to garnish

Bring a large saucepan of water to the boil, and add the fusilli with a dash of olive oil. Cook for about 10 minutes, stirring occasionally, until tender. Drain, return to the saucepan, and set aside.

Arrange the chunks of pepper on a baking sheet, and place in the broiler for about 5 minutes, or until slightly charred. Preheat the oven to 400°F.

Mix the pepper into the pasta with the remaining ingredients, and toss together to combine. Transfer to an ovenproof dish and bake for about 15 minutes, or until heated through and the cheese has melted. Sprinkle with the chopped parsley, and serve.

Cheesy Pepper Supper

Based on the traditional macaroni and cheese, this colorful, tasty supper is a great dish for kids.

SERVES 4–6

2¼ cups dried macaroni

½ red pepper, deseeded and finely diced

½ yellow pepper, deseeded and finely diced

dash of olive oil

FOR THE SAUCE:

¼ cup butter

½ cup all-purpose flour

2½ cups milk

2 tsp French mustard

scant ½ cup grated Cheddar cheese

salt and freshly ground black pepper

FOR THE TOPPING:

1 cup fresh breadcrumbs

¾ cup grated Cheddar cheese

YELLOW

Bring a large saucepan of water to the boil, and add the macaroni with the diced peppers and a dash of olive oil. Cook for about 10 minutes, stirring occasionally, until tender. Drain and transfer to a shallow, ovenproof dish. Set aside. Preheat the oven to 400°F.

To make the sauce, melt the butter in a large saucepan, then stir in the flour to make a paste. Gradually stir in the milk, a little at a time, until evenly blended, with no lumps.

Gently bring the sauce to the boil, stirring constantly, until thickened. Stir in the mustard and cheese and season with salt and pepper. Continue to cook for a further 1–2 minutes, until the cheese has melted.

Pour the cheese sauce over the macaroni and pepper mixture, and mix it in with a spoon. When the sauce and pasta are evenly combined, sprinkle with the topping ingredients and bake for 25–30 minutes, until crisp and golden.

Gnocchetti Sardi with Broccoli and Tomatoes

A lovely light lunch or supper dish. Choose vivid green, tightly packed heads of broccoli, and cook as briefly as possible to retain the color and crisp texture.

TARRAGON

SERVES 4

¾lb dried gnocchetti sardi (small dumpling shapes)

dash of olive oil

⅓ cup unsalted butter

¾lb small broccoli florets

1 clove of garlic, chopped

2 tsp chopped, fresh rosemary

2 tsp chopped, fresh oregano

salt and freshly ground black pepper

7oz can chopped tomatoes

1 tbsp tomato paste

fresh herbs, to garnish

Bring a large saucepan of water to the boil, and add the gnocchetti sardi with a dash of olive oil. Cook for about 6 minutes, stirring occasionally, until tender. Drain and return to the saucepan, covered, to keep warm.

Meanwhile, melt the butter in a large frying pan. Add the broccoli, garlic, rosemary and oregano, and season with salt and freshly ground black pepper. Cover and cook gently for about 5 minutes, until tender.

Add the chopped tomatoes and tomato paste, and stir. Add the gnocchetti sardi, mix together lightly, then serve immediately, garnished with fresh herbs.

Buckwheat Noodles with Savoy Cabbage

Buckwheat noodles, known as "pizzoccheri," are a specialty of northern Italy, and are available from some Italian delicatessens. Wholewheat or egg tagliatelle make good substitutes.

SERVES 6

¾lb dried buckwheat noodles

½lb savoy cabbage, shredded

1 medium potato, peeled and diced

dash of olive oil

½ cup plus 2 tbsp unsalted butter

2 cloves of garlic, chopped

4 tbsp chopped, fresh sage

pinch of freshly grated nutmeg

scant ½lb diced Fontina cheese

1⅓ cups freshly grated Parmesan cheese

Bring a large saucepan of water to the boil, and add the buckwheat noodles, cabbage, and potato with a dash of olive oil. Cook for 10–15 minutes, stirring occasionally, until tender. Drain and set aside, covered, to keep warm.

Meanwhile, melt the butter in a large frying pan, and sauté the garlic and sage for about 1 minute. Remove from the heat and set aside.

Place a layer of the pasta and vegetables in a warm serving dish, and sprinkle with a little nutmeg, some of the Fontina cheese, and some of the Parmesan cheese.

Repeat the layers, then pour the hot garlic butter over the pasta. Mix lightly into the pasta and serve immediately.

Gnocchetti Sardi with Broccoli and Tomatoes.

Pasta-stuffed Cabbage Leaves

Easy to prepare and sure to impress the guests, this dish can be made the day before and kept in the refrigerator. Allow an extra 15–20 minutes to reheat in the oven before serving.

TORTELLINI

½ cup dried gnocchetti sardi (dumpling shapes) and/or pastina (any tiny shapes)

dash of olive oil

8 large savoy cabbage leaves, stalks removed

FOR THE FILLING:

2 tbsp olive oil

2 cloves of garlic, crushed

2 carrots, peeled and grated

2 zucchini, grated

4 tomatoes, skinned, deseeded, and chopped

½ cup chopped walnuts

salt and freshly ground black pepper

FOR THE SAUCE:

14oz can chopped tomatoes

4 tbsp dry red wine

⅔ cup vegetable broth

1 tbsp dried oregano

1 onion, very finely chopped

salt and freshly ground black pepper

Bring a large saucepan of water to the boil, and add the pasta with a dash of olive oil. Cook for about 10 minutes, stirring occasionally, until tender. Drain and set aside.

Blanch the cabbage leaves in boiling water, then quickly immerse in cold water and drain. Pat dry with paper towels, and set aside.

To make the filling, heat the olive oil in a large frying pan and sauté the garlic for about 1 minute. Add the grated carrots and zucchini, and cook for a further 3–4 minutes, stirring occasionally, until tender.

Add the chopped tomatoes, walnuts, and pasta. Season with salt and freshly ground black pepper. Cook for about 5 minutes, stirring occasionally, then set aside to cool.

To make the sauce, place all the ingredients in a saucepan and bring to simmering point. Cook for 20–30 minutes, stirring occasionally, until reduced and thickened. Allow to cool slightly, then transfer to a food processor or blender and purée until smooth. Set aside. Preheat the oven to 400°F.

To assemble the stuffed cabbage leaves, lay the blanched leaves out on the work surface, concave side uppermost, and divide the mixture between the leaves, placing it in the center of each. Fold the edges of each leaf over to completely encase the filling, securing with a toothpick.

Arrange the stuffed leaves in a shallow ovenproof dish, and pour the sauce around the edges. Cover with aluminum foil and bake for about 20 minutes, until heated through. Serve immediately, with any extra sauce served separately.

Cannelloni with Greens and Walnuts

Serve with a simple, crisp, fresh salad to complement the rich, cheesy sauce and walnut filling. Fresh spinach is a good alternative for this recipe.

SERVES 4

12 dried cannelloni (tubes)

dash of olive oil

butter, for greasing

½ cup walnuts, chopped

FOR THE FILLING:

3 tbsp olive oil

1 large onion, chopped

1 clove of garlic, crushed

1lb mustard greens, shredded

7oz can chopped tomatoes

1 tsp dried oregano

3 tbsp chopped, fresh basil

½lb ricotta cheese

1 cup fresh whole-wheat breadcrumbs

½ cup walnuts

good pinch of freshly grated nutmeg

salt and freshly ground black pepper

FOR THE CHEESE SAUCE:

2 tbsp butter

¼ cup all-purpose flour

1¼ cups milk

⅔ cup grated Fontina cheese

Bring a large saucepan of water to the boil, and add the cannelloni with a dash of olive oil. Cook for about 10 minutes, stirring occasionally, until tender. Drain and rinse under cold running water. Drain again, then pat dry with paper towels and set aside.

BASIL

To make the filling, heat the olive oil in a large frying pan and sauté the onion and garlic for 2–3 minutes, until the onion has softened. Add the mustard greens, tomatoes, and oregano. Continue to cook for about 5 minutes, stirring frequently, until the liquid has completely evaporated. Remove from the heat and leave to cool.

Place the mustard greens mixture in a food processor or blender, and add the basil, ricotta cheese, breadcrumbs, walnuts, and nutmeg. Purée until smooth, then season with salt and freshly ground black pepper.

To make the sauce, melt the butter in a saucepan. Stir in the flour and cook for 1 minute. Gradually stir in the milk, and heat until bubbling and thickened. Stir in the grated Fontina cheese.

Preheat the oven to 375°F. Butter the insides of a shallow, ovenproof dish. Using a teaspoon, stuff each cannelloni with the filling, then lay it in the dish.

Pour the cheese sauce evenly over the cannelloni. Sprinkle with walnuts and bake for about 30 minutes, until bubbling and golden.

TIP:
Sheets of fresh lasagne can be used instead of dried cannelloni. Make up ½ quantity Pasta Dough (page 8), and roll out to ¼ inch thick. Cut into 4 × 6 inch rectangles, and spoon some of the filling along the short end of the sheet of pasta. Roll it up into a neat tube, and place in the dish with the sealed end underneath.

Tagliarini with Green Beans and Garlic

A delicious summer salad, hot main course or vegetable accompaniment, this dish is suitable for almost any occasion.

ROTELLE

SERVES 4–6

¾lb dried tagliarini (flat spaghetti)

dash of olive oil, plus 4 tbsp

¾lb green beans

1 medium potato, cut into ½-inch cubes

3 cloves of garlic, chopped

5 tbsp chopped, fresh sage

salt and freshly ground black pepper

freshly grated Parmesan cheese, to serve

Bring a large saucepan of water to the boil, and add the tagliarini with a dash of olive oil. Cook for about 10 minutes, stirring occasionally, until tender. Drain and set aside.

Cook the beans and potato cubes in a large saucepan of boiling water for about 10 minutes, until tender. Drain well, and set aside to keep warm.

Heat the remaining olive oil in a large frying pan, add the garlic and sage, and season with salt and freshly ground black pepper. Sauté for 2–3 minutes, then add the cooked beans and potato. Cook for 1–2 minutes, then add the cooked tagliarini and mix well.

Cook for about 5 minutes, stirring occasionally, then transfer to a warmed serving dish. Sprinkle with freshly grated Parmesan cheese and serve.

Fettuccine with Garlicky Creamed Spinach

This tasty recipe is quick and easy to prepare. Serve immediately with plenty of freshly grated Parmesan cheese.

SERVES 4–6

1lb dried fettuccine

dash of olive oil

2 tbsp butter

3 cloves of garlic, crushed

1lb frozen chopped spinach, thawed and well drained

1¼ cups light cream

pinch of freshly grated nutmeg

salt and freshly ground black pepper

⅔ cup freshly grated Parmesan cheese, plus extra to serve

Bring a large saucepan of water to the boil, and add the fettuccine with a dash of olive oil. Cook for about 8 minutes, stirring occasionally, until tender. Drain and set aside, covered, to keep warm.

Melt the butter in a large frying pan and sauté the garlic for 1–2 minutes, then add the spinach. Cook over medium heat for about 5 minutes, stirring frequently, until the moisture has evaporated.

Add the cream and nutmeg, and season with salt and freshly ground black pepper. Toss in the fettuccine and Parmesan cheese, stir, and cook for a final minute. Serve with extra freshly grated Parmesan cheese.

Asparagus Ravioli with Tomato Sauce

A dinner-party dish which can be made in advance – the ravioli can even be put in the freezer several weeks before and cooked from frozen. The sauce can be made several hours ahead and reheated before serving.

SERVES 6

⅔ quantity Pasta Dough with 1 tbsp tomato paste beaten into the eggs

1 quantity Tomato Sauce

1 egg, beaten, for brushing

dash of olive oil

chopped fresh herbs, to garnish

FOR THE FILLING:

2 tbsp olive oil

1 clove of garlic, crushed

1 onion, very finely chopped

½lb fresh asparagus, very finely chopped

salt and freshly ground black pepper

Keep the fresh pasta dough covered with plastic wrap at room temperature, and the Tomato Sauce in a saucepan, ready to reheat before serving.

To make the filling, heat the olive oil in a frying pan and sauté the garlic and onion for about 3 minutes, until the onion has softened. Add the chopped fresh asparagus, and season with salt and freshly ground black pepper. Sauté the asparagus mixture for about 10 minutes, until softened. Set aside and allow to cool completely.

To make the ravioli, cut the pasta dough in half. Roll out one half to a rectangle slightly larger than 14 × 10 inches. Trim the edges of the dough neatly. Cover the rectangle with the plastic wrap to prevent it drying out. Roll out the other half of the dough to the same measurements. Do not trim the edges.

Place half teaspoonfuls of the filling mixture in lines, spaced about ¾ inch apart, all over the trimmed rectangle of pasta dough. Lightly brush the beaten egg in lines around the filling mixture, to make the square shapes for the ravioli.

Lay the other rectangle of pasta dough on top and, starting at one end, seal in the filling by lightly pressing the dough, pushing out any trapped air and gently flattening the filling, making little packets. Using a sharp knife or pastry wheel, cut down and then across in lines around the filling to make the square ravioli shapes.

To cook the ravioli, bring a large saucepan of water to the boil and add the ravioli with a dash of olive oil. Cook for about 6 minutes, stirring occasionally, until tender. Drain and set aside.

Meanwhile, reheat the Tomato Sauce. Serve the ravioli with the Tomato Sauce, sprinkled with chopped fresh herbs.

ASPARAGUS

Lentil and Coriander Lasagne

You could make up two or three portions and freeze them uncooked. They cook beautifully from frozen at 375°F for 50–60 minutes.

SERVES 1

⅓ cup red lentils, washed and drained

1 onion, roughly chopped

2 cups boiling water

1 tbsp olive oil, plus extra for greasing

1 clove of garlic, crushed

3 tbsp chopped, fresh coriander

¼lb mushrooms, sliced

2 tsp sweet soya sauce

1 tbsp tomato paste

salt and freshly ground black pepper

1 sheet fresh lasagne (approx 8 × 4 inches), cut in half

½ quantity Cheese Sauce

⅓ cup grated Cheddar cheese

Place the lentils and chopped onion in a large saucepan, and add the boiling water. Bring to the boil, then simmer for about 15 minutes. Drain and set aside. Preheat the oven to 400°F.

Heat the olive oil in a large frying pan and sauté the garlic and coriander for about 1 minute, then add the sliced mushrooms. Cook for about 4 minutes, then add the sweet soya sauce and tomato paste, and season with salt and freshly ground black pepper. Add the cooked lentil mixture, stir, and cook gently for about 5 minutes.

To assemble the lasagne, oil a shallow ovenproof dish and place one sheet of the lasagne on the bottom. Cover with half the lentil mixture, then add the other sheet of lasagne. Spoon the remaining lentil mixture over the top, spread out evenly, then pour the Cheese Sauce over the top. Sprinkle with grated cheese, then bake for about 20 minutes.

> **TIP:**
> This is a perfect opportunity to use up any leftover homemade pasta from another recipe – it is not worth making up a fresh batch for this dish since it uses such a small amount.

ROTELLE

Corn and Butter Bean Bake

Canned beans are ideal for this recipe, so take advantage of their convenience.

FARFALLE

SERVES 4

1 cup dried farfallini (tiny bows)

dash of olive oil

3 tbsp sunflower oil

2 cloves of garlic, crushed

1 onion, very finely chopped

3 tbsp chopped, fresh thyme

4 sticks celery, chopped

8oz can butter beans, drained

1 cup frozen corn kernels

1 tbsp wholewheat flour

1¼ cups vegetable broth

salt and freshly ground black pepper

FOR THE TOPPING:

2 tbsp sesame seeds

2 tbsp fresh wholewheat breadcrumbs

sesame oil, to drizzle

Bring a large saucepan of water to the boil, and add the farfallini with a dash of olive oil. Cook for about 8 minutes, stirring occasionally, until tender. Drain and set aside. Preheat the oven to 350°F.

Heat the sunflower oil in a large frying pan and sauté the garlic, onion, and fresh thyme for about 3 minutes, until the onion has softened.

Add the chopped celery and cook for about 3 minutes, then add the butter beans and corn. Cook for about 5 minutes, stirring occasionally, then stir in the flour until evenly blended.

Gradually stir in the vegetable broth, stirring well, then season with salt and freshly ground black pepper. Cook for about 5 minutes, then transfer the butter bean mixture to a shallow, ovenproof dish.

In a small bowl, combine the sesame seeds with the breadcrumbs, then sprinkle the mixture over the butter beans. Drizzle a little sesame oil over, then bake for about 20 minutes, until the topping is crisp. Serve immediately.

Sautéed Flageolet Beans with Fusilli

A garlicky dish, made with fresh tarragon to enhance the delicate flavors. Serve as a main course or as an accompaniment.

SERVES 2–4

3½ cups dried fusilli (short twists)

dash of olive oil, plus 4 tbsp

3 cloves of garlic, crushed

1 large onion, sliced

2 tbsp chopped, fresh tarragon

14oz can flageolet beans, drained

salt and freshly ground black pepper

Bring a large saucepan of water to the boil, and add the fusilli with a dash of olive oil. Cook for about 10 minutes, stirring occasionally, until tender. Drain and set aside.

Heat the olive oil in a large frying pan and sauté the garlic and onion for about 5 minutes, until the onion has browned slightly. Add the tarragon and beans, and season with salt and freshly ground black pepper. Cook for 2–3 minutes, then stir in the fusilli. Cook for 3–5 minutes, to heat through. Serve with a crisp green salad.

Winter Stew

You can give this vegetarian dish to carnivores – they'll never notice the lack of meat.

SERVES 4

1½ cups dried wholewheat radiatori (radiators)

dash of olive oil, plus 2 tbsp

2 cloves of garlic, crushed

1 onion, chopped

5–6 carrots, cut into ½-inch chunks

½lb button mushrooms

14oz can chopped tomatoes

2 × 14oz cans red and black kidney beans, drained

1¼ cups vegetable broth

1 tbsp paprika

2 tbsp sweet soya sauce

salt and freshly ground black pepper

1 tbsp cornstarch

KIDNEY BEANS

Bring a large saucepan of water to the boil, and add the radiatori with a dash of olive oil. Cook for about 10 minutes, stirring occasionally, until tender. Drain and set aside.

Heat the remaining olive oil in a large saucepan and sauté the garlic and onion for about 3 minutes, stirring occasionally. Add the carrots, and cook for about 5 minutes.

Add the mushrooms and continue to cook for about 3 minutes, stirring occasionally, until slightly softened. Add the remaining ingredients, except the cornstarch, and stir in the radiatori. Cover, and cook gently for about 15 minutes, until the vegetables are tender.

In a small bowl, mix the cornstarch with a little of the cooking liquid to make a smooth paste. Add the cornstarch paste to the stew. Stir and allow to boil again, stirring constantly, until thickened. Cook for a final 3 minutes before serving.

Sautéed Flageolet Beans with Fusilli.

Continental Lentil Soup

Canned lentils make this soup even easier to prepare. They are available from most good delicatessens.

FUSILLI

¼ cup butter

2 cloves of garlic, crushed

⅓ cup dried pastina (any tiny shapes)

4 tbsp finely chopped, fresh parsley

14oz can brown lentils, drained

6½ cups vegetable broth

salt and freshly ground black pepper

freshly grated Parmesan cheese, to serve (optional)

Melt the butter in a large saucepan and sauté the garlic for about 2 minutes, stirring occasionally.

Add the pastina and chopped parsley, and stir. Cook for a further 2–3 minutes, then add the lentils and stock, and season with salt and freshly ground black pepper.

Bring the soup to the boil, then reduce the heat and simmer for about 15 minutes. Serve with a little freshly grated Parmesan cheese, if wished.